REBUILDING LOVE AS A COUPLE

A THOUGHTFUL GUIDE TO MONOGAMY, ROMANTIC LOVE, AND SEXUALITY

JENNY PAOLA OSORIO ECHEVERRI

CAROLINA CARDONA

Translated by
LINA MARIA PINEDA CARDONA

GUÍA PARA
SER HUMANOS
EDITORIAL

Dear Reader,

We appreciate the time spent reading this book and hope that it will be useful in your life as a couple. Preferably, if you are in a relationship, it is recommended that it be read by both of you, since in this way you will be able to discuss the contents and learn about how social phenomena cohabit in the relationship.

CONTENTS

REBUILDING OTHER WAYS OF LOVING

INTRODUCTION

From childhood to adulthood, human beings' lives are immersed in imaginaries, projections, and symbols related to love as a couple. Family, school, and other socialization contexts, linked to traditional media and social networks, teach through themselves the ways of expression in sex-affective relationships, presenting monogamy articulated to romantic love and heteronormativity as the prevailing, homogenized, and normalized way of assuming love as a couple in society.

In this book, love as a couple is approached from a critical and reflexive perspective, specifically supporting three fundamental pillars that, according to our perspective, are the ones that compose it: monogamy, romantic love, and sexuality. This is with the intention of unveiling how these pillars work in the current sex-affective relationships and also with the purpose of deconstructing generalized ideas about "love as a couple" that circulate and are reproduced without being reflected upon in our society.

The processes of deconstruction of a couple's love are necessary and fundamental to understand under which mental and social schemes we human beings are operating in our relationships. But also, to reconstruct other types of sentimental bonds in which the recognition of the partner predominates without self-annulment, allowing us to understand and accept the other as a socially constituted being with stereotypes and modeling, just like us. Likewise, this deconstruction makes possible the reduction of self-criticism and judgments within the relationship and towards other people who decide their sex-affective relationships in a monogamous way and in other ways too.

Therefore, "Rebuilding Love as a Couple: A Thoughtful Guide on Monogamy, Romantic Love, and Sexuality" provides readers the possibility of acquiring different and alternative strategies for improving their personal capacities as well as romantic relationships, allowing them to become healthier, more flexible, more understanding, and less conflicted.

LOVE AS WE HAVE BEEN TAUGHT

Love Since the Greek Times

There are different ways of loving and love. In modernity, our language functions as a kind of barrier, limiting us to recognizing other conceptions of love and thus not being able to give it different meanings. That is why we tend to use these two ideas (loving and love) to refer to almost any relationship in which a kind of affection arises.

As with other concepts, love did not escape our "primitive" search to explain, through myth, the reality we experience. Greek mythology characterized different types of love with their respective particularities, giving way to a new experience of feeling. The most important categories of love for the Greeks would be called Philia, Storge, Agape, and Eros.

The first three types of Greek love would include feelings of cooperation; emotions associated with friendship; brotherhood; concern; affection for others; love for the whole; for nature; and for the magnificence of the universe. However, Eros, the subject of this book and god of love, is related to carnal affairs and intense love, which needs this bodily closeness to subsist.

Eros is responsible for the sexual attraction and passions of all mortals. Perhaps knowing his origin will help us understand what love meant to ancient Greek society. Eros was the son of Aphrodite and Ares, that is, a son of the goddess of love and beauty and the god of war. This duality is easy to recognize since, in our relationships, we constantly feel this displacement between conflict and pleasure.

For the Greeks, love was a divinity, a strange being with superior qualities capable of causing madness and foolishness, even to the wisest human being. They believed love was a kind of passional load that invaded, flooded, and controlled us; it was a trap, a wound to the heart, but it was also that bittersweet taste of life with elusive notes of magic and happiness. Because of this feeling, great heroes and feats have been formed and countless battles have been fought. As the old adage would say, "all is fair in love and war".

By means of this, we want to show that the view of Western love under which we have built our understanding of this feeling and we have sown the expectations that motivate us to experience it is totally permeated by that supreme Eros that Greek history and mythology teaches us. Greece, the cradle of Western civilization, established the frameworks within which we now live romantic love, which has become a business, a necessity, a duty, but also an essential way of relating to one another.

The Social Construction of Love

Being in love, getting into a relationship, getting married or living together with another person, whom we call a partner, has become a generalized and common experience in our society. Likewise, it is common to hear or go through processes of breakups and mourning that leave us in pain due to the strong emotions that this generates, but also with the longing to finally find the person who will accompany and love us for several years in a constant way.

To this extent, being in a couple is one of the most normal and customary ways of experiencing and projecting life, which is why it is one of the most significant desires human beings have during their existence. However, this does not happen just for the sake of it, nor is it a transmission from generation to generation that occurs in a purely natural way.

Human beings have the capacity to create and transmit what has been previously constructed to other people. Here we will dwell specifically on the subjective creations of the mind that allow us to interpret and understand the world. Just take a look at the complex social realities that society has woven. For instance, it is very likely for you, for us, and for many people, that family is one of the most important aspects of life. But why do we share this? Society, through the family itself, along with other institutions such as educational and religious institutions, has taught us this way of significance towards it. Therefore, we understand and feel it as a fundamental element in our lives.

That is to say, all that we live, understand, and feel about family is a creation of the human person that, when taught and shared by other people, becomes a social construction that is transmitted culturally among generations and in different contexts. For instance, we do not know each other, but in spite of this, in such deep significance, we have things in common, such as thinking and feeling that family is a fundamental element. This is because we are permeated by these social constructions that go through us from the external to the most intimate.

The family issue is used to exemplify human-social constructs, how we share them, and how they influence us in this existence. Love as a couple doesn't escape either from being a social construction that has taught us and led us to certain feelings, beliefs, and behaviors. That is to say, love as a couple is a way of feeling and experiencing life, created by human beings, that has become generalized as a way of relating among people. If it were not so, why do couples' relationships look so much alike? Of course, there will be differences between each couple, but each one shares some characteristics that are learned about how to be a couple. Otherwise, how can we differentiate between a couple's relationship and a friendship or family relationship? There are specific elements that a couple shares, and these are the ones that delimit us if we are in a romantic relationship or not (review the pillars of love section).

Love between partners, like many other social constructions, whether pleasant or unpleasant, is learned through interaction with other people. This is how we acquire aspects without wanting or looking for them. A human being has the capacity to create and destroy. Each one, as a particular subject, can develop the ability to build and deconstruct other elements that contribute to that loving world that is desired. It is important that this new configuration of the space in a couple that is going to be created is stripped of some of those social learnings that tend to distort and limit this sharing with each other.

Recognizing that couple relationships have this social component that runs through us and influences us in the aforementioned way allows us to know when we are falling into learned patterns that may not contribute favorably to the loving relationship we are trying to establish. All in all, there are elements that condition us to be and act as we do, but there are some of these that lead to establishing toxic relationships; aspects that are better to unlearn, to create a different way of experiencing and living the so-called and so longed for love as a couple. To this end, throughout the book, as in the section "The Pillars of Love" and in the chapter "Deconstructing the Idealization of Love", you will find elements that will allow you to understand what it is, and how to deconstruct the love as a couple that we have been taught and that we have learned throughout our lives.

To sum things up, romantic relationships are part of a social construction that has been transmitted historically in different contexts and to each one of us as one of the most significant ways of relating to each other and living adult life. The longing for this type of relationship, plus the difficulty of creating and assuming a different way of being "in a couple", shows how we are tied to social structures that guide us, but at the same time it is difficult for us to let go of them.

CHAPTER I: THE PILLARS OF LOVE

Love as a couple, which we have been taught is based on three fundamental pillars: monogamy, romantic love, and sexuality, will be expanded on below.

First Pillar: Monogamy

Monogamy and Capitalism

The current economic system and private property are based on the relations of production and are responsible for giving a social and economic order to our reality, thereby regulating important aspects of our lives such as the legal organization, the state, and the family. The last one is a symbol of our modern and "civilized" culture because it is a small unit endowed with authority that contributes to the current economic and sexual order.

The monogamous-heteronormative family has a structure that is based on economic and not natural conditions (Engels, 1980:68). It reproduces itself by perpetuating behaviors of sexual repression to prolong the productive and reproductive cycle as well as to avoid social judgment. We can observe this in our recent history. For example, in the twentieth century, dominant class families suppressed their daughters' sexual freedom, valorized their "virginity," and finally, gave them as merchandise to a certain family or to the highest bidder, in order to maintain future commercial transactions and/or increase their patrimony.

This example is used to show that family, monogamy, and capitalism constitute property and ownership, and as a consequence, limits are established. These limits are attached to sexual rights, making them exclusive and minimizing the emotional freedom of individuals. It becomes a matter of owning and being owned.

We agree in part with scholars who claim that the birth of private property is the beginning of stricter sexual norms, especially for women, as they continue to be socially restricted and punished when they decide to break the "rules." We also agree when they state that the orientation towards private property eternalizes marriage-monogamy-patriarchy cycles, the latter due to the social and economic predominance of men in the family.

Monogamy is a pact that is generally not agreed upon, but it is taken for granted. Thus, we do not intend to say that monogamy is a good or bad form of relationship. Beyond this, we are interested in people questioning this concept, which has become the social glue for couples, and deciding whether to keep it or not, with a little more freedom and consciousness.

Monogamy as a Political Issue

Practicing monogamy is a common and ordinary fact. Doing so does not make someone more or less. Ignorance of what revolves around this way of relating does not mean that the choices of being in a couple do not have implications in the social context we inhabit. Every time we choose to have a couple relationship, we are aiming at principles of possession and privacy, which are ultimately subservient to the economic, social, and political systems that govern us today. In this sense, we become political beings that contribute to normalizing and consolidating the social organization in which we live.

That's right, you are a political being whether you like it or not, or you feel indifferent to it. Monogamy is shown as a way of relating to each other, but deep down it has a high political content and origin because it leads us to a lifestyle of doing, acting, feeling, and thinking. That is to say, it models us around the project required to sustain a prevailing social organization.

For monogamy to be exercised, it needs actors, which in this case are people. In this sense, when we decide to be in a couple, we are assuming not only a way of creating an affective bond but also some norms, beliefs, and economic-political principles that allow us to belong and apparently fulfill ourselves in a social order.

As a political being, it is very likely that you are contributing to sustaining capitalism in many ways, despite the criticism and resistance that you may or may not give. From the decision to relate to each other as a couple, we are bringing to our intimacy a complex political world that crosses us all. Recognizing these undercurrents appears to complicate couple relationships more than they appear to be. However, they are deep elements in which each of us moves, and it is necessary to identify them in order to approach them in more sincere, authentic, and less utilitarian ways of loving the other.

Monogamy and Ego

Little by little, we have been overcoming the discourse that maintains that monogamy is a biological matter, something natural and intrinsic to human beings and other animals. We can still hear some voices arguing that it is unnatural to love two people at the same time and to maintain more than one sexual-romantic relationship, although these voices have less echo each day. On the other hand, more and more people understand and talk about love as a social construction, a construction that is linked to monogamy in order to maintain the economic and cultural order, and as individuals immersed in it, it is difficult not to be conditioned.

However, this book is **NOT** intended to convince the reader as to where he or she should stand in the debate, nor does it wish to enter into the realm of "right" and "wrong" or "good" or "bad." Beyond this, we seek to show that there may be one or more ways of interpreting reality, trying to avoid the duality that arises between biological and social construction. We intend a deeper reflection that goes beyond this debate, which in a certain way has limited us to knowing and accepting ourselves more humanely.

As we have mentioned above, in monogamy, two aspects of private property are perceived; they are two sides of the same coin: a possessor and a possessed. It seems that in love relationships, there is an egotistical need to possess the other and a desire to feel possessed, turning the other into another property. The enunciation to ratify the right over the other is given by the language when using phrases such as "**My** girlfriend/boyfriend," "**My** husband/wife," "**My** friend," etc.

Jealousy is usually that emotion or reaction that clearly evidences the fear of losing that property, which can lead to ego pain. How can I understand that my partner desires and can enjoy another person sexually and emotionally? We have found in our psychosocial consultations that for many people, pride (ego) becomes a pain-avoidance mechanism that prevents them from releasing the other person from that possession. As a reflection of this, we have heard phrases like: "First I have to leave her, then she can leave me," or "It's not going to be so easy for that other one!" These expressions show one ego trying to put itself before the other.

In ego-based relationships, it is common to see how the concept of love is more about one's own needs than about the relationship or the partner. They are two subjects attracted by their narcissistic desires with the expectation that love is certainty, and this is where monogamy and ego fit in, since they seek to be the partner's **only** and **exclusive** object of desire. With the desire to acquire a guarantee of a lasting and forever love, they hope to find peace of mind in the possession of the other, ceding the satisfaction of their desires and the responsibility for the achievement of their "happiness" to the partner of the moment. Once this magical idea and fabricated story by the ego is over and the relationship is broken, a new cycle begins over again where two egos interact with each other, reproducing the social construction of falling in love.

Second Pillar: Romantic Love

Romantic Love as a Social Mechanism

The Argentine philosopher Sztajnszrajber sustains romantic love as a mechanism that conditions people's behaviors, feelings, and thoughts in their socio-affective relationships. The decisions and expressions we make are based on the ways we have been culturally taught or told about romantic love, which is generally as a couple.

Think of different couples or remember how your love relationships have been. It is very possible to identify in them the same signs of affection, for example, dedicating songs with similar lyrics or even dedicating the same ones, giving roses, eating in a special place, etc. Also, when saying "my love," "my life," or other ways of naming your partner, what they ultimately intend is to symbolize and represent exclusivity.

All of this is done in the hopes of eliciting memories, being important to the other person, and strengthening affective bonds. But let's notice that in spite of changing partners and even if there are different partners in our environment, we operate in love relationships in the same way through the device of "romantic love," "love as a couple," or "falling in love." Although we try to vary or be authentic, it is usual to fall into the predetermined patterns that have told us what it is and how to be in love.

Society is a transmitter of knowledge and culture, and each of us is a being that learns and is constituted through socialization. The transmission of culture is usually associated with scientific knowledge, customs, and traditions. It is essential to transcend this conception to a deeper look that allows us to dimension how society, through culture, creates adequate or inadequate ways of feeling and relating, which we assume, integrate, and replicate in our actions. Culture exercises the function of directing, but it is also responsible for limiting and conditioning other possibilities of bonding, emotional and relational creation. This is what happens when we feel, think, and experience love as a couple. The fact that the same type of relationship is repeated among so many people is not a coincidence, nor less natural.

Romance

Romantic love has become the modern utopia for not "suffering" from loneliness. Under this idea, we have accepted an old story that has taught us to think and feel love as a couple in certain ways, where both men and women have accepted socially expected conditions and behaviors that have prevented us from experiencing love in simpler and freer ways.

Romance is related to the idea of romantic love, which is an idealization or a fiction in which we hope that, especially sexuality, love and commitment converge and are articulated in the same being. The satisfaction of social, personal, intimate, and even economic objectives acquires a character of dependence exclusively on another, thus consolidating an imaginary about the partner or the loved one: to be a complement that facilitates the realization of those personal desires.

The expectation that the partner will provide friendship, economic association, sexual enjoyment, and leisure space, among other things, becomes an ideal that projects certainty to the human being. However, in this materiality, it can be a frustrating search because it is complex that all these elements are manifested and realized through another and also a single subject. Precisely, these are the expectations that have been created from the existing social constructions of love as a couple, which we assume as certain or true in our ways of creating personal bonds and which distort and limit our relationships with each other and even with ourselves.

It is precisely in this confused elaboration of love, observed under the veil of romance, that certain behaviors we have naturalized or believe to be typical of being in a couple are justified. Attitudes such as jealousy, blackmail, excessive surveillance, the imposition of giving up things, activities or important personal relationships, disguise violence and the need for possession under the mask of romantic love.

In relation to these learned behaviors, we can give as an example heteronormative romantic love, in which men have been taught that romance makes more sense if there is difficulty in the conquest ritual. Furthermore, in the insistence of achieving the object of their passion, they could validate themselves through the label of "success" with women. On the other hand, as women and in articulation with the behaviors expected from men, historically we have been imposed the patriarchal model in which "feminine" subtlety is used to please physically and receive compliments, in addition to the excessive importance of the first sexual act and the desire to be a wife and a mother.

Third pillar: Sexuality

Sex and Love

We can agree that sex and love are fundamental aspects of life in the present materiality, at least for most people. These two issues enjoy a "normal" presence in our realities, invading us with enriching experiences, multiple learning and delicious hormonal stimuli. Of course, both concepts have also taught us other strengths, such as acceptance and renunciation, through breakups, separations, and personal differences.

Sex and love are concepts commonly confused and mixed with each other and with others. It should be remembered that sex is submerged within three perspectives: biological, anatomical, and social sex. Biological sex refers to the genes or genetics that each human being receives at the moment of gestation. Anatomical refers to the external sexual and reproductive organs, while social sex/gender, perhaps the most contentious today, refers to the role that people are assigned based on their biological sex. On the other hand, we have sexuality that arises from the interconnection between sensuality and genitality, in a ritual aimed at obtaining pleasure. Our sexuality generally moves between three motivations: romantic, ludic, and reproductive.

However, the transmission of feelings through sexuality from a romantic motivation is of great importance for the enjoyment of sexual expression since it builds trust, bond formation in the couple, a sense of exclusivity and feelings of permanence with the other, etc. For this reason, it is relevant to discover and understand the analytical/social part of sexual relations. With regard to sexuality and love, a kind of ideology has been fabricated, produced, and reproduced: we have been taught what it is about, how it is done, with whom it is appropriate to do it, when to do it, for what purpose, as well as the space it should occupy in every human being's life. Sexuality has become a model that has determined us, and in this same function, with the same arguments, we have determined others.

Sexual love is the combination of conditioning about sexuality and love. In this sense, sexual love is a romantic way of calling for sexual pleasure or intercourse. This type of love often unquestionably reproduces the idea that having a partner guarantees a sexual act and that every sexual act done with the partner is an act done with love.

After stopping at a social view of sexuality and love in order to understand a broader version of these concepts, we consider it necessary and fundamental to mention that we can achieve more sincere, satisfying, and frank types of sexual love relationships.

It is important to recognize that this type of relationship, whether we want it or not, will be marked by common and recurrent ways of acting and feeling, such as idealization, commitment, tenderness, desire, and empathy, among others. Undoubtedly, we are and will be immersed in this when we talk about love as a couple. Nonetheless, the search will continue towards a rethought and reflected idea of love and sexual intimacy, which is flexible and adjusted to the needs, particularities, and interests of each couple's member, so that each one can unite with the other without getting lost in him/her or in the ideas that modern society has continually presented to us.

The Modeling of Human Sexual Intimacy

The reproductive act, what is known as "having sex," has received other meanings captured by the invention of romantic love, since talking about sex in modern times and being in a couple does not mean having sex but making love. That is to say, sex, besides being enjoyed, must be experienced with love, taking on a deep meaning and significance for the individual, leaving him/her entangled in a lot of expectations and meanings that he/she must both expect and at the same time fulfill. Expectations about this physical sexual act as a couple become a transcendental aspect that can unite or separate couples.

Recognizing that we move under the model of fulfilling and satisfying the expectations of the sexual act as a couple can help us understand that sex develops and is entangled in sexual duties that we integrate as indispensable without being aware of it. By talking about duties, we are opening up what is appropriate and inappropriate (what should and should not be or be done), thus becoming norms to follow in the sexual act. Just when we decide to regulate our courtship or marriage with these rules or regulations around sexuality and sex, we are reaffirming and allowing the modern social modeling of our sexual behaviors and beliefs.

From this perspective, "having sex" and "sexuality" are not the same. The first refers to the act itself and the second to different sexual manifestations of the human being, which can range from sexual orientation to gender identity, among others. Although they are different, both have points of convergence. The way sexuality is assumed to govern the way of living sex. In this sense, sex is crossed by other meanings of the subject with respect to his/her own body, corporeality, and object of desire.

Sexuality integrates one's own corporeality and that of the other; the way of perceiving and assuming it is neither free nor totally autonomous from each subject. On the contrary, it is tied to socially learned forms that indicate how to experience sexuality. The greatest example is heteronormativity, which places heterosexuality (taste for the opposite gender, man-woman, and woman-man) as the generalized and "normal" sexual orientation, denying other possibilities of sexual preferences. This heteronormativity brings with it other norms, since in addition to indicating that you should like a person of the opposite gender, it also directs how a person should behave socially according to his or her sexual organ.

The experience of sexuality is then allowed, but in certain and limited ways. For this reason, Foucault maintains that sexuality is not repressed but modeled. This modeling occurs for utilitarian purposes, which will contribute to the maintenance of the economic and political system that governs society. For labor, people are required to reproduce, and for this reason, heterosexuality is the best allied and pertinent sexual orientation for this purpose, since fertile men and women are the ones who make procreation and industry possible.

Despite the fact that this is a comprehensive, critical, and reflexive perspective on sexuality that allows us to understand at a societal level the aspects that interweave and compose us as subjects, it is unquestionable that we move internally under these representations, as this crosses us in our feelings because it has a deep meaning for us. Sexuality brings together energies, sexualities, and life experiences that give meaning to human existence.

Although we are socially and politically modeled, our encounters of pleasure are important because it is the nudity of the body that is present there, converging and sharing with the other's sexuality.

The feelings that arise around it are fundamental because they guide and give meaning to life.

With the critical perspective exposed in the previous lines, we do not intend to minimize or undervalue sexual experiences. On the contrary, we consider that they are fundamental because they integrate who you are and your way of living this human experience. The proposal we make is oriented to reflecting on one's own sexuality, from what pleases us and what does not, in order to strip little by little of pre-established social schemes.

Tensions Triggered by the Pillars

Exclusivity (monogamy), romantic love and sexuality, are the central axes that support couple relationships, which as mentioned in the previous section, are incorporated in our relationships in a silent, hidden way, without being perceptible to the naked eye.

In this way, they have another interesting side to deepen; just as they are a fundamental basis for the sustainability of a relationship, they are also creators of tensions in the dynamics of the couple and in each personal world that composes it.

To understand what we mean by these tensions, it is important to say that these three pillars, being constructions of society and learned by every human being, imply aspects that shape our feelings and beliefs in the way we relate to each other as a couple.

Therefore, they become regulating principles and, at the same time, limiters of who we are and how we live our lives, both publicly and privately with regard to the couple.

Monogamy, romantic love, and sexuality are regulators because they are elements that indicate what is okay to do and what is not okay to do as a couple. This regulating and delimiting function creates tensions between what we desire and what we should experience.

In this way, the pillars are configured as standards that allow us to compare and specify what the relationship is, as well as to determine whether or not it is working.

For the couple, the fulfillment of the pillars is stressful because they are composed of standards, idealizations, expectations, and limitations, which become aspects that must be manifested harmoniously and simultaneously within a relationship.

Therefore, when some aspect does not work as it "should," we look for it to be fulfilled according to the expectation that being in a couple generates. Below, we propose an explanation of how these pillars' tensions work:

PILLAR	Tension Manifestations	Perception	Implications within the Couple's Relationship
Monogamy When a person establishes an exclusivity agreement with another person, he/she is bound by implicit rules, among which there is a fundamental one: there is no room for third parties; "we are only two because this is the way a couple is constituted."	Jealousy	The other is perceived as one's own, as an object that is possible to possess and that belongs to us	1. It creates an expectation that the other will correspond to an exclusive love. 2. The other is distorted by the expectations and the established agreement, since the other is seen as an object that can be possessed, managed, and manipulated. 3. Duties are attributed to the couple that restrict personal expression due to fear of loss, justified by love, camouflaging the possession and abuse of rights attributed to the other. As an example, restriction of privacy, social ties, forms of personal expression such as clothing, ways of speaking, socialization, etc.

PILLAR	Tension Manifestations	Perception	Implications within the Couple's Relationship
Monogamy	Physical and emotional violence	The other is perceived as his own, as an object that is possible to possess and that belongs to him/her. In this sense, the other is seen as less deserving. "When he/she doesn't do what I want, I need to control him/her."	1. The use of force or symbolic forms to assert one's supposed superiority. 2. Manipulation of the situation to make one party believe they are inferior and the other superior in order to keep the relationship going. 3. Complex and violent forms of relationships that are difficult to resolve are created. ***All these implications hinder the parties' personal development.***

PILLAR	Tension Manifestations	Perception	Implications within the Couple's Relationship
Romantic love A relationship of dedication, commitment, sensitivity, and emotional connection is idealized.	Love-sentimental stereotypes	It is believed that one is the center of the couple and that one must satisfy romantic and emotional expectations. It is inferred that there are specific ways of expressing love and being a partner. When the standard is not met, the love that the other person claims to feel is doubted.	1. I does not allow the expression of one's own and the partner's particularities. 2. There is little understanding of the other person's particular ways of being and expressing him/herself emotionally. 3. It is expected of the other person to fulfill one's own expectations about the couple's behavior. 4. He/she is rigid.

PILLAR	Tension Manifestations	Perception	Implications within the Couple's Relationship
Sexuality Sex is captured by romantic love; hence the sexual act is called "lovemaking". In this sense, it falls into line with standards of how the sexual act should be experienced as a couple. On the other hand, sexuality is modeled; it indicates how it is to be lived and what roles are established in the couple's bond.	Stereotypes on sex and sexuality	It is believed that sex must be done with love and that sexuality can only be fully experienced with a partner. The partner is expected to comply with the monogamous sexual bond, with a specific sexual orientation and gender identity, and to behave according to the standards that these imply.	1. It conditions the sexual act and sexuality to be expressed in certain ways. 2. It confines the characteristics of each sexuality to a specific social role. 3. Incomprehension and inflexibility become elements of the relationship that limit the possibility of emotional and sexual connection between individuals. It also restricts the couple from finding new ways to live their sexuality.

The expectation of full compliance with these pillars leaves us exposed to failure and frustration, because, as can be seen, there are many aspects that are at stake and that must be satisfied at the level of each subject and the couple. For this reason, the expectations created by these pillars of relationships can generate tensions that can lead to common and major conflicts in the couple.

The purpose of presenting you with these tensions is to help you reflect on how the principles you subscribe to as a couple mobilize you into feelings and limitations that prevent you from establishing different dynamics within relationships. It is extremely complex to escape from these pillars. However, the management that we give to the tensions can be the beginning of managing the relationship differently through particular ways that each relationship creates, through understanding but at the same time deconstructing these social aspects that limit them, taking into account the history of the relationship as well as the ways of being, feeling, and acting of each member of the couple.

Other Deep Reflections on What We Have Been Taught About Love

So far, we have made a very brief description and analysis from a critical-comprehensive perspective on the pillars on which we have been taught to love: monogamy, romantic love, and sexuality. We have mentioned at a historical level how the concept of love has been transformed from the Greeks to the present day. In addition, we expressed how these pillars have led us to a social re-organization that is supported by marriage and the family, meaning these as small administrative units that collaborate with the productive and reproductive social order.

It has also been mentioned that from our most intimate parts, which include the body, our desires, and sexuality, we have been somehow "modeled" by a cultural or social phenomenon. We, on the other hand, find ourselves as subjects in these same conditionings because they provide meaning to our affective experiences and human existence. Furthermore, during this chapter we have recognized the importance of love (existing since the world has existed), we understand that it is part of our emotionality and of a biological-chemical-neuronal process, and we try to know a little about how we experience this feeling in modernity.

But this is not all. Anyone could then say: "I understand that love and all its variants have a history, a transformation, a utility and, by the way, many pleasures. I understand that, but we already love these ways; we have become used to it and it is okay; nothing is going to change." The truth is that everything on the whole has implications. That is, from the perspective we propose, the ego, neoliberalism, the current economic system, the social imperatives of sexuality, the family, and contemporary social organization have a direct relationship with love and how it has been configured and will continue to do so.

In other words, at this point, we wish to put certain questions to tremble in order not only to understand love from a rational point of view, nor to try to create an ideal and much less perfect one, but to review it articulated to what has been mentioned about it and perhaps to reach a glimpse of a love as authentically human as possible.

What we are trying to share with you in this section could be summarized by the following premise of the South Korean philosopher, Byung Chul Han: love is currently threatened with death. He tells us this in his book "The Agony of Eros", where he takes up the problems of the current era, such as hyper-modernity that implies hyper-consumerism. This reflection is related to the concept of Liquid Modernity (2004) developed by the sociologist Zygmunt Bauman.

This hypermodern society has spawned and carries on its own afflictions. It has been known to transform certain diseases of past times, but it has also created some new ones. Chul Han tells us about the symptoms of this contemporaneity: the excess of narcissism (or ego?), depression, anxiety, guilt, and the excess of positivity (dealt with in his book "The Burnout Society"). This last concept refers to that well-known way of life: I can; "I can do everything in this life and I must avoid failure, I must think positively, etc." This excess of "self-motivation" results in self-control and self-exploitation, a role previously embodied by an external agent (commonly a boss) and now performed by ourselves.

So, we have that the sum of narcissism, positivity, and all the psychosocial consequences that arise from it, have love in a checkmate. Why? Because narcissism or the excess of love for oneself has disappeared or destroyed that other who accompanies me or will accompany me in the process of the relationship, we melt in our ego, denying the other and refusing to open ourselves to him/her.

As an example, we could refer to the characteristics and/or biotypes of personalities and bodies that we see, long for, and seek as possible partners. We want our partner to be tall or short, thin or fat, and also like the same music, agree on a movie genre, and have a liking for X or Y pet, etc.

After finding the "right" person and passing through the phase of falling in love, it is very common to realize that this person has some peculiarities that we do not particularly like. She is messy, doesn't take care of her finances, expects something different from me about the future, is not very detail-oriented, doesn't laugh at my jokes, etc. All this evidences how we move under narcissistic elements, trying to make the other adjust and conform to my tastes or be like "me." That is where Chul Han tells us that this is not love but consumerism, or in his own words, when otherness is stripped from the other, one cannot love—one can only consume (Chul Han, 2012:13). This author adds that this narcissistic condition of today's society is closely related to the new power schemes.

On the other hand, the excess of positivity is what makes us "be able" and "achieve" more and more things, it is knotted to optimistic phrases that tell you that "if you want to, you can" whose subliminal message is: if you couldn't it is because maybe you didn't want so much or you didn't try hard enough. In the pursuit of our "goals," combined with the structure of today's society, we have entered an underworld that keeps us busy seeking to generate income to have a life we could not otherwise have and a lifestyle stereotyped by the media and advertising. While we are in this situation, we do not have a lot of free time because in this self-exploitation, as B. Chul Han points out, we have, for instance, to work overtime and/or get an additional job. This fact then causes a kind of abandonment of the partner and other people close to our social circle.

As we said earlier, monogamy is a strong ally of the capitalist system since it allows people to take economic and emotional responsibility for a family, maintaining and reproducing this social organization. But, in addition, it preserves in the subjects enough energy to support and produce in a job for at least 8 hours and return home to "procreate" and satisfy family demands. However, the time devoted to the family and other close social bonds after a working day is not enough or what we would like, and unfortunately, it is not enough time for love, because, as the Argentine philosopher Juan Denis would say, love cannot reach its fullness without some leisure time. In the excess of positivity, there is a denial of failure, and in this lack of negativity, love also suffers. Therefore, there has proliferated a fear of commitment, of falling in love, and above all, of the wound of love.

Another element that does not escape the consumerism in which we are currently immersed is sexuality. The sexual act has entered the circle of performance, commodification, and exploitation through pornography. With all this, we have transformed "having sex" into a pastime and the other one into a sexual object available for consumption, stripping the sexual act of eroticism.

In summary, according to what has been discussed in the book so far and with the philosopher Byung Chul Han's support, a small radiography has been generated on how and why Eros is threatened with death and how this deep wound has stripped it of its content.

Even though it is difficult to recognize these reflections approached from a critical-social point of view, these are aspects that very probably manifest themselves in our society, in your family, in your partner, and in you. Although it is complex to propose a specific solution to the problems generated by the pillars of love as a couple, we consider that it is possible to deconstruct this type of love that we have experienced up to now. For this reason, in the following chapters we propose some questions to rethink your way of establishing the bond as a couple.

DECONSTRUCTING THE IDEALIZATION OF LOVE

CHAPTER II: HOW DO WE IDEALIZE LOVE?

Plato and His Idea of Love

Forever—ancient and recent times—different ideas and explanations have been developed about the nature of love, for this subject has occupied a prestigious place in the studies of the most renowned philosophers, and, of course, it is an almost universal topic for the rest of us mere mortals. The common interpretation that has been given to the view of love by the famous Plato of Greece, apprentice of Socrates, has not escaped our misunderstanding.

Much has been written and said about "platonic love", a type of "love" that many people claim to have experienced once in their lives: it is an unrequited love, idealized, unrealized, surely impossible; a lofty and sublime love, however, lacking in something, in physical contact or mutual attention. The use and reuse of the concept has led us to repeat these things without even bothering to read about their origin.

To clarify, we want to say that one thing is the Platonic love that we use daily in everyday life to refer to those ideal loves, and quite another is the perspective of love that Plato intended to show us in his dialog "The Banquet." But where and why has this confusion arisen?

We maintain that it all starts with a misreading of Plato, together with a need to pigeonhole love as we want it to be. We seek a lasting or eternal love. We look for "the love of our life", but we also want this love to always feel "beautiful", to give us wellbeing, to be beautiful, strong and robust in the face of difficulties, difficulties that we do not want to see appear.

On the other hand, we desire and seek the perpetuation of our "self" through another being. How? This is usually done through physical reproduction since children are often the means to give the continuation of our being through genes, the dissemination and propagation of our memories and experiences to achieve immortality on this physical plane, even if we do not know what we are seeking.

Besides the perpetuation of our being through children, we seek to immortalize ourselves through our loved ones. We want to be that person who will never be romantically forgotten, to be someone's "love of life," the special human creature with whom that other person does things he or she would never do alone or with anyone else.

All this seems to be very beautiful, but it was not what Plato sought to share. For this philosopher, Eros was not a supernatural being, of irrational and divine force, as some of his Athenian aristocratic characters in the text "The Banquet" affirmed in their speeches. A dialogue above all others, which reveals his vision of the nature of love, is precisely the discussion between Socrates and Diotima.

The notion of these two characters places love on a different scale than the one it had been given since it seeks to give a more spiritual and less physical or sexual notion of love. According to them, Eros was not a god, but neither was he a mortal being. He was "something halfway" between both extremes and, moreover, he was the child of two opposite poles: Poros (abundance) and Penia (poverty). With this, we notice, as we did in the first section of chapter one (Love since the Greeks), that for the Greeks, love is a mixture between bliss and suffering, between having everything and having nothing. That is to say, their argument fits perfectly with the way we live love in the West, which, however, seems to be a reality that we find difficult to recognize as we pretend to always feel intoxicated and satiated by love, refusing to accept that, as love is abundant, one day it also dies and disappears.

Going back to Plato, Diotima, and Socrates, they make an exposition of the nature of love by elevating it to the sphere of beauty. Eros served as an intermediary, or "something halfway," between mortality and immortality, a link between the divine and the human realm; he did not possess beauty; thus, he desired it; that is, he desired it precisely because it is something he did not possess. This desire is not just any desire, but a particular one, since it is the desire to possess "something" forever. This would explain why love manages to be preserved in romantic relationships since, even if we "keep" a partner, the thought that he or she is not "ours" completely will always be present as long as there is a reasonable doubt that he or she may walk away someday.

For Socrates, according to the dialogue written by Plato, love is "the desire for the eternal possession of the good." In other words, to possess beauty. But what is beauty? According to this philosopher, beauty is what would allow us to approach immortality and to be gods. This assertion allows us to ask why humans want to be gods, and the answer could be simply: because we are mortal! Love is desire. Desire will always be what we will always lack: immortality, even if we are not ready for it.

We agree with Plato when he argues that we seek the perpetuation of our being in the material and historical plane we occupy. For mortality aims at the disappearance of the "self" at a given moment. His perception of how we seek to immortalize our being, on the other hand, transcends the physical, sexual, and reproductive planes where we tend to settle, and it is here that we have misrepresented his concept of love.

For Plato, beauty—love—goes beyond perpetuating the species to which we belong or ourselves, but consists in the gestation, multiplication, and reproduction of ideas in other souls and/or minds, in order to immortalize ourselves, but not conceiving of the couple or children as the only means. It is possible to walk the path to love described by Plato to achieve beauty and happiness through the transmission of ideas or knowledge in different areas, such as art, writing, sports, and, of course, other people different from the partner and children.

In Search of the Better Half

In our current society, there is a widespread belief about love: that there is a right person for each of us. In this belief, it is conceived that for every human being, there is someone who fits almost perfectly into every type of taste (physical, sexual, and personality). But in addition to this, it is believed that with this same person there is a close, intimate and indissoluble emotional connection, so much so that it can be thought that they are soul mates or the love of life.

The question is how not to think about it. If the media and social contexts in which we move show us this, since it is usual to see on websites like YouTube or social networks videos about how to find the better half or our complement, Also, it is common to hear phrases in the middle of a love loss to encourage us, like "the right person for you will come along" or to ask ourselves "when and where will the right person for me appear?"

These are phrases and sayings that show that we believe that there is only one person in the world for each of us and that the rest of the experiences with other partners with whom we have not lasted and there has not been a great emotional connection, are love failures that indicate that they were not our complement and that the search continues for him or her, because somewhere has to be found.

However, when we believe that we have found our "better half," but this person leaves our lives, we feel incomplete, empty, emptied, meaningless and without the will to go on with life. Something quite similar is exposed in the myth of the androgynous that Plato exposes in his aforementioned book "The Banquet". In this text, the androgynous is revealed as a being with one head and two faces, four legs and four arms, and is shown as two human beings joined by the back and belly. The androgynous were beings constituted by a man and a woman, also a woman-woman and a man-man.

It is said in the book that they were beings with great strength that managed to threaten the power of the Olympian gods, to which Zeus responded by throwing lightning on the androgynous, causing the separation of them into two (in half). Since then, these beings have wandered through life in an endless search for meaning to their existence: to reclaim the half from which they were separated. When this reunion did not happen, these beings entered a state of deep sadness that could even lead them to death.

It is intriguing that so many years ago, there were so many similar ideas about love as we now conceive and live our love experiences. As we mentioned at the beginning of this book, what we have learned about love is influenced by interpretations of Western positions that are supported by philosophical ideas coming from Greece. Talking about the better half implies going back to the Greek philosophers, because until today, their ideas and the interpretations surrounding them continue to endure.

To this day, Plato lives on and is immortalized by his ideas. We still talk about him and continue to analyze his texts. It could be argued that we live love looking for "our complement" in the same way that androgynous people looked for their other half after their separation caused by Zeus. And it is possible that we find aspects that reaffirm it, since it is fundamental for the current human being to find someone with whom to share his life; this is one of the most significant searches during his existence, to which he designates time, effort, and dedication, in spite of it not always turning out as desired.

The ideas of love that currently circulate in our society are learned from other people, either because they are erroneous interpretations that have been given to relevant exponents or because it is something that the social environment reinforces for us from history. However it has happened, our material and subjective experience of love is strongly influenced by the conception of love in complement, of the better half or of a missing half.

It is complex to disassociate oneself completely from this idea, but it is relevant to think of oneself outside of being and feeling incomplete, why? Because these beliefs will cause you to move away from the lack, you will believe that you cannot be or be calm if you are not in the company of a partner. It is possible to feel good without being with a partner, although sometimes you may think it is not. What happens is that to achieve it requires unlearning behaviors and beliefs that we have learned socially.

Regardless of how you choose to assume and live your life (as a couple, with several lovers, or alone), from this section of the other half, we want the reader to question and dismantle these recurrent beliefs of the complement in the other, ideas that sometimes we think we do not have but are there expressing themselves in different ways in our desires and thoughts about love.

It is important that you give yourself the opportunity to rethink yourself from another place, one that allows you to redefine yourself as a sufficient and complete individual, whether in company or alone, and also allows you to feel and redefine the other detached from the need and emotional deficiency.

Love and Falling in Love: Different or Similar?

Love is a subject about which we all believe we know and have a truth. It is usually that this happens when, in one way or another, we have all had love experiences that give us authority to talk about it and discuss it.

Many of the conversations about love that arise in everyday life usually show ideas and beliefs that are shared in common about being in love and loving. Two in particular stand out:

- Loving and being in love are the same thing.
- Loving and being in love are two different things.

Which position do you identify with more? On the websites and people who write about these topics, they are emphatic about the differences between love and falling in love. That is to say, they tend to support the idea that they are two different aspects.

Since it is explained that both are phases but that falling in love is previous to love and that each one is lived and felt in a different way, the following is a simple summary of the explanations given about the differences between falling in love and loving someone:

Falling in Love
↓

It is a chemical-hormonal process that lasts for a period of time during which we are moved mainly by emotions.

↓

Which are its characteristics?

To see only what is positive and pleasant about the person.

Emotions run high; there is a strong excitement and anxiousness to share with the person you like.

↓

Associated behaviors and feelings
↓

-Wanting to spend the whole time with that person.
-Feeling that time goes by when you are with him or her.
-Sensation of "tingling" or butterflies.

Love
↓

It is a process of choice that is sustained over time, with thought predominating over emotions.

↓

Which are its characteristics?

The flaws and qualities of the loved one are perceived, seeking to provide understanding.

Emotions are less intense and show fluctuations.

↓

Associated behaviors and feelings
↓

-Understanding the partner's time and space.
-Plans are projected together.
-There is no rush, there is confidence about the commitment established within the relationship.

These differentiations about love and falling in love that circulate on the internet can be useful to try to understand and categorize our emotions when it comes to sharing our life with another person. However, these appraisals fall back on standards since, if we believe in them, they delimit our actions and feelings within love relationships, limiting and biasing not only our feelings but also those of our partner. But this does not only happen to those people who conceive of love and falling in love as different. Since people who think of them as equals do not escape stereotyping in their own relationships.

People who believe that these two concepts are the same, as well as those who conceive them as different, tend to adopt very specific criteria about love and falling in love, develop love relationships categorized by inflexible standards, and establish adequate and inadequate ways of giving and receiving affection.

Because of this, when there is a thought or a feeling that is out of the norm, the relationship enters a state of alert because it is questioned and doubted, tossing back and forth on whether to keep the romantic bond or end it. When the infatuation phase is over, a common example—explaining it in terms of someone who perceives love and falling in love as equal—occurs because the person starts to think that because they are no longer experiencing the intense excitement, their feelings have changed, and there is no longer any love.

In this way, we reduce our relationships to the socially created canons of love and submit them to the judgments established and legitimized by themselves. Then, we are predominantly hooked on the two beliefs initially exposed about love and falling in love (whether they are the same or different). Nevertheless, it is possible to create other beliefs and conceptions of all the human experiences that we have developed around love as a couple.

We take up common beliefs and general explanations about love and falling in love because we believe it is critical to expose the social constructs through which we are sexually and affectively relating to each other. Likewise, we make this approach to evidence the longing that we human beings have to preserve an emotional state for an extended period of time. However, because the human being has become used to certainty, which is very understandable, it is essential to dimension love and/or falling in love as feelings that transit, that is to say, that are not preserved in the same way as at the very beginning. The understanding of this serves to avoid clinging and getting attached to standardizations, which in the long run can cause us discomfort and suffering when the established criteria of how we are told and how we expect love or falling in love to manifest itself are not fulfilled.

Love and falling in love are different ways of referring to human affective sexual experiences, which are widely complex due to their various hints, and it is important to accept them from their highest peaks to their middle and lowest ones. Otherwise, we are forcing our relationships to fit into what is said "should be" and what should be sensitively experienced as love. In the same way, we are exposing ourselves to vulnerability since sustaining what love and falling in love should be becomes a social and, at the same time, a personal demand, which when not fulfilled generates frustration and a sense of failure.

Let us recognize that regarding relationships, it is possible to experience pleasant sensations and emotions as well as others that are not or not so pleasant. Regardless of the connotation we give them, these feelings are part of the experience that will allow us to appreciate and accept humans from the exploration of love as a couple. With this, we also allow ourselves to free ourselves to a certain extent from social canons that are imposed on us, and at the same time, we impose on ourselves.

Falling in love (as presented in mind map # 1) shows us how personal satisfaction is above that of the other, because we want to consume the person we like at all times. From the philosophical perspective, this is not the meaning of love, because in love what matters is the other, that is, the partner's satisfaction and not the personal one. The author Correa, in the text "La deconstrucción del amor como imperativo ético" [The deconstruction of love as an ethical imperative], tells us that when love is an exchange, a contract and a market relationship are created, since to expect the other to attend to and satisfy us is to deny the other and to super-impose our own individuality. Moreover, this selfish act is to empty love itself of its meaning. Following this same line, there are philosophical authors such as Correa and Sztajnszrajber who share with us an idea of love in which detachment from one's own desires and devotion to the other is fundamental to demercan-tilizing and resignifying the act of love.

Resignifying Love-Eros is an act that corresponds precisely to the couple, since it is there where we accept behaviors that stereotype and reproduce imaginaries about love. Resignifying implies thinking more deeply about what we do, think, and feel in order to identify what can be substantially changed and, at the same time, to create other ways of living love. Are you and your partner in a position to resignify yourselves and elaborate on a different love or loves?

Culture Teaches Us Love: Music As a Mechanism

During the drafting of this book, we have mentioned several times that the issue of love—a universal and controversial topic—has been the subject of study and sociological research that argues that love is part of a social construction in which we are immersed. From this perspective, it is supported that there are specific cultural mechanisms that influence and fulfill certain functions in the normalization of attitudes, actions, thoughts, and reasoning about romantic love.

Within these mechanisms, we find resources that allow its cultural reproduction, such as music, literature, novels, movies, and so on; all of these are articulated with traditional media such as newspapers, television, and radio, as well as with the newest and most frequently used media, social networks.

All of this can be better understood if it is placed within a historical context, since the types of music and novels that people in our current society watch or read did not appear out of nowhere. Societies change as history is woven, which is created according to their circumstances. Thus, it could be summarized that modern society was forged under the project of the Enlightenment (18th century). This European intellectual movement is the protagonist of important social changes, and from this arises the cultural movement called Romanticism, which questioned (but did not deny) the rationalist interests of the Enlightenment, also pursuing human freedom as an ideal, but also proposing the revaluation of feelings (ignored by the Enlightenment). In other words, romanticism hoped to find a harmony between sensibility and knowledge, the basic elements of the human being.

Romanticism exalted creativity, imagination, and feeling, permeating art and literature with its romantic discourse. Poetic creations proliferated in Europe, and literary changes were noticeable, with chivalrous themes, violent scenes, women as objects of desire, and the need for courtship being addressed. These facts influenced social relations and the interaction between the couple's relationships.

From this short recap, we could argue that today's society inherited, interpreted and restructured certain connotations about love coming from the romanticism movement, but this fusion between new and old conceptions of romantic love has been merging to the interests of capitalism through commodification, conceiving love as a consumer good. Sex and love are elements constantly used by the advertising industry to sell—and we buy—products or services, although love is more subtly marketed and sex is more moralized.

Love has been commercialized through music, literature, and audiovisual media. Although they are artistic expressions, many continue to perpetuate and excuse certain behaviors as something "natural" in love. Jealousy, emotional attachment, physical and symbolic violence are just some of these. Nothing about love is natural, because it is a concept that has been influenced by the cultural and ideological ideas that have been interwoven around it.

Next, we will focus on music as a mechanism by which modern society advertises love to us.

Music

Have you ever wondered what percentage of music talks about love or heartbreak? We have asked ourselves this question without finding any reliable scientific research that can answer it. However, we dare to affirm that most of the lyrics of current music are composed under these two axes (love and hearthbreak). All of this is added to the fact that it is increasingly difficult to establish auditory barriers to sound stimuli since we hear romantic songs in the supermarket, in the store, in the neighbor's house, in the street, making it complex to visualize the normalization that has been made of them since music is constantly around us with few possibilities to control and select it.

The most serious aspect of this situation is that we do not cultivate the habit of filtering the information that comes through music (and other media), as we usually listen to it in the background, or unconscious of its content, while we are enjoying our leisure time, doing our work, and/or doing our homework. This unconscious listening automatically evokes our emotions, of which we do not yet have a better understanding and enough self-control.

A song might not be able to change the world, but Héctor Fouce, a writer and musicologist, claims that 50 years of songs that recycle models and clichés have contributed to the common sense we now take for granted. " Music has the power to create meanings and symbols in physical materiality and multiply them in the collective unconscious. Through songs, standards of how a couple should be, sexist ideas about the roles of men and women, love is idealized, or, more accurately, the ideal of love and the feelings culturally and socially associated with it are hyperbolized. Phrases such as "without you I cannot live", "I need you like sunlight", "without you I am nothing" and "true love forgives" are sung at the top of our lungs without reflecting on how dangerous the ideas we are "swallowing" can be for ourselves.

We would like to quote a real-life example, with due consent, in order to show how music influences people's lives. One of our patients, whose love relationship was deteriorated by the psychological and physical abuse of her partner, decided one day to end that relationship while she was traveling abroad. There, she tried to create a new life by getting a new job and joining a new social support group. Despite her efforts to end the relationship, she had phone contact with her former partner, who dedicated a very emotional and sensitive song to her in these approaches, instilling in the patient the fantasy that this "love" was the "love of her life," the predestined one, and that it could change or improve if both of them intended it, because "love can do everything." It was a matter of days before our patient returned to her native country to continue with her idyllic love, leaving behind opportunities and new experiences. Instead, she decided to prolong for approximately two more years that distorted "love" that from beginning to end was characterized by issues of abuse and violence.

The songs' subjects are usually related to an ideal of love, a betrayal, a victim's or victimizer's version of "love", resentment or desires for suffering towards the former partner, and other distorted ideas of love and sex as a couple. Although reggaeton has been attributed mainly to sexual violence issues because it is more explicit and direct, the truth is that many songs of all musical genres have and have had sexist content, as some songs normalize and promote sexism and sexual harassment.

Lyrics such as the following:

·Dime que No:

"Si me dices que sí, piénsalo dos veces, puede que te convenga decirme que no. Si me dices que no, puede que te equivoques, yo me daré a la tarea de que me digas que sí"

"Dime que no, me tendrás pensando todo el día en ti, planeando la estrategia para sí" – Ricardo Arjona

This song's lyrics serve as an apology to sexism, which elevates and normalizes stereotyped and misogynist attitudes. Additionally, it also seeks to justify the conduct of thousands of violent men and even depicts the loss of restraint and reason as a romantic ideal.

· Propuesta indecente:

"Si te invito a una copa y me acerco a tu boca, si te robo un besito, a ver, ¿te enojas conmigo? ¿Qué dirías si esta noche te seduzco en mi coche? Que se empañen los vidrios y la regla es que goces. Si te falto el respeto y luego culpo al alcohol, si levanto tu falda ¿Me darías el derecho a medir tu sensatez? - Romeo Santos

The fragment of this song reflects some situations of harassment and abuse that women have experienced and may experience in public spaces, especially at parties where there is psychoactive substance consumption. It also shows how, through music, these types of actions are manifested, which apparently appear flirtatious and harmless because they are usually justified by courtship and alcohol consumption, but deep down they reveal violence and violation towards the other and specifically towards the female body by not considering her consent and desire as important.

The purpose of this section is not to undervalue music or other types of artistic expression, but rather to promote awareness of the importance of establishing a filter for idealizations of love, songs, movies, novels, books, and social networks, since they are the most effective means of absorbing information. The responsible consumption of literary, audiovisual, and digital resources supports the construction of healthier social relationships, the strengthening of self-esteem, and refines the ability of critical-social reflection.

CHAPTER III: COMMON LOVE PHRASES SCRUTINIZED FROM MONOGAMY, ROMANTIC LOVE, AND SEXUALITY

In this section, we will focus our attention on phrases about love that are usually used and heard among people, which by being common are conceived as normal. However, behind them are hidden meanings that affect, influence, and determine the construction of our identity. Therefore, the approach to these phrases is relevant and is carried out in order to understand and unveil precisely these hidden meanings. For this purpose, we will use a structure based on the pillars that support love (monogamy, romantic love, and sexuality).

Monogamy and its Phrases

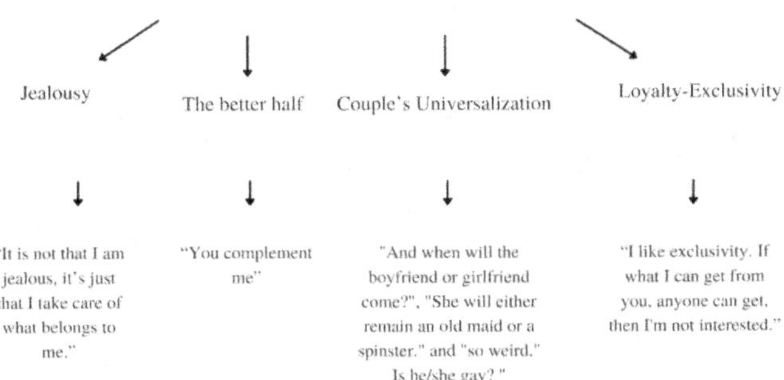

Jealousy

Emotions are important from any point of view. They constitute psychological phenomena proper of any person. They allow us to understand behavior and the human experience. Since the majority of any human being's transcendental thoughts, behaviors, and social relations occur as a result of some emotion or in anticipation of experiencing one.

Emotions arise from the exchanges that a person has with his or her environment, in those interactions that are sustained with others in different social contexts. In these exchanges, "negative" or "positive" emotions arise, according to the judgment that each person has about the situation that happens to him/her, that is, if he/she considers the circumstance he/she is facing to be threatening or if, on the contrary, it is exciting or motivating.

This implies that emotions are mediated and saturated by the meanings that each person assigns to them, and that they are influenced by the social environment in which they exist. Some emotions will have a positive or negative connotation depending on the cultural environment, since this produces the scripts that guide individuals to expected social behavior.

In this sense, emotions fulfill certain social functions, such as contributing to sustaining the cultural value systems of X or Y region or society, but they also facilitate the creation, conservation, and dissolution of social relations.

Jealousy is one of the most complex human emotions, and it's also one of the most common, perhaps more than we realize, because who hasn't been affected by a situation in which jealousy was present and obvious? In relationships between siblings, friends, and employees, this emotion is common when possibly seeking the approval of an authority figure.

Some authors, such as Plutchik, refer to jealousy as the fusion or mix of anger and fear, two usually basic emotions. Others define it as a feeling halfway between fear and hate, and some as a combination of fear, anger, and love.

Depression, envy, aggression, anguish, paranoia, distrust, threat, anxiety, desire for revenge, outrage, insecurity, guilt, anguish, obsessive thinking, social comparison, and, in short, enormous emotional and sometimes physical pain can result from these intertwined emotions, which appear to be triggered by a supposed "rival."

Source: Reidl, L. Celos y envidia, emociones humanas (2005)

Although jealousy can be felt or caused by any type of social relationship, it is nevertheless a subject commonly associated with romantic relationships. This emotion is generally caused when one of its members perceives the real or imaginary threat of losing the relationship or the loved one, usually to another person.

Because we recognize that as sentient beings, we can experience various types of feelings and emotions, our approach seeks to understand the human being by distancing ourselves from judgments of their emotions. However, it is important for us to highlight the social normalizations that have been created around jealousy and what lies behind it. For this, we will analyze a phrase that is recurrently used in social contexts:

"It is not that I am jealous, it's just that I take care of what belongs to me."

The previous statement is usually heard and reproduced by members of romantic relationships that excuse feelings of inferiority, search for social validity, and need for possession of the romantic love they claim to have. For many people/couples, jealousy is a fundamental element of "true love", since the absence of jealousy "evidences" a clear disconnection and lack of interest from the loved one.

In this aspect, attempts are made to control and preserve exclusivity/fidelity above and beyond what is necessary, acquiring selfish and repressive behaviors such as invasion of privacy, restriction of socializing with other people, criticism of personal interests and dressing styles, among others, in order to protect the person as a possession. On the other hand, the practice of power and control as the fundamental basis for the couple's cohesion often becomes a mechanism or device for physical and gender violence and crimes committed in the name of romantic love.

In short, jealousy:

- Is not a synonym for love.
- It does not justify violence.
- It is not wrong to feel it, although we must be aware that there are mental and social structures such as monogamy and exclusivity that lead us to get confused and create this emotion in us. When jealousy appears, it creates an opportunity to identify those parts of our being that must be reconsidered in order to carry out introspective work with them, which allows us to improve as individuals and in our interactions with others.

As we mentioned before, emotions can create, preserve or dilute social-love relationships, and specifically, jealousy has serious consequences that can range from compromising communication, trust, self-esteem of both partners, or permanent separation.

The Better Half

The ideal couple that the media tries to "promote" to us is easily recognized as the "better half." In this ideal, love is understood as an encounter between two incomplete beings; an apology and a deceitful hope to reach completeness are built. So, in the illusion of this type of romantic love, there are two halves of an orange that were predestined to meet and fit together, ready to join and become a single orange. Although one is not necessarily equal to the other (belief of "opposites attract"), each feels that without that other half, it is totally incomplete. Once they meet and are mated to each other, they can live happily ever after.

The most representative phrase of the idea of the better half in our society is **"You complete me,"** which is a romantic way of affirming that without that person, our life is incomplete. However, perfect complementarity does not exist because as much as a person can "understand" or "couple" with another, and types of beliefs such as that they are "made for each other" are given, the reality is that this is not enough to sustain a healthy relationship.

Independent people, on the other hand, who cultivate their emotional skills through effort, dedication, understanding, patience, and many other factors, have a better chance of achieving a balanced relationship, understanding that they are responsible for themselves and that they are autonomous individuals with the ability to make their own decisions.

Couple's Universalization

In the society we live in, it has become a general belief that everyone has had, has or will have a partner. That is why it is common in social gatherings to come across phrases addressed to those people who break this imaginary, saying: "**And when will the boyfriend/girlfriend come?"** Or in very specific cases when it is a woman, **"She will either remain an old maid or a spinster."** And for men, we hear **"so weird, is he gay?"** This is evidence that not having a partner is socially sanctioned differently for women and men, calling into question, respectively, the ability to bond sexually and affectively or the person's sexual orientation.

Such phrases hide an idea that most of us share: we believe that having a partner is an essential element in human beings' lives, so when someone does not have one, it is either strange or inconceivable to think of ourselves without one. Likewise, these phrases and imaginaries hide a symbolic violence for each one of us since they constantly expose us to judgments and questioning from others about our personal decisions to share or not share life with another being. In this sense, having a partner becomes a social requirement that, when we do not comply with it, punishes us or even generates feelings of frustration for not sustaining a loving relationship.

That is to say, having a partner functions as a generalized requirement in our society that has implications for every human being, creating an attachment in beliefs of approval towards monogamous bonding and, with this, generating feelings of urgency and need to acquire it or feelings of failure for not having it. This allows us to understand why we sometimes use these types of phrases and also the consequences they have on each person's mind. Likewise, to understand the importance of not reproducing phrases that lock us to social demands, constructed and accepted by ourselves. Let us allow ourselves to open the cage in which we have locked ourselves. One way to do this is by respecting the different manifestations of being that break with what is expected and what we believe to be appropriate in our way of relating to each other.

Loyalty and Exclusivity

Human beings need certainty in the economic, labor, and relational fields in order to feel secure and at ease. In the economic and labor aspects, certainty is sought because it provides a means of subsistence in this world, and in the relational aspect, it ensures accompaniment and protection.

When the economy and relationships are articulated, generalized social dynamics arise, especially focused on maintaining exclusive relationships, helping to save time and energy, which will be used in different activities of economic production, allowing us to exist in this materiality. These dynamics are prevailing in our current society. Therefore, the love plane cannot escape these structures and certainty becomes a mechanism for protection.

Exclusivity, then, does not arise for its own sake, nor as a whim, but because of the urgency of protecting one's own certainty. In this sense, exclusivity and certainty are two linked words, which allow us to understand that in both there are fears and insecurities of material and subjective loss. There is an obvious two-part composition in a couple relationship, with the need for exclusivity standing out; thus, the approach of a third party or other outsider to the relationship poses a risk not only of rupture, but also of loss of emotional, affective, and economic certainty.

The human being's need for certainty demonstrates a denial of its counterpart: uncertainty. This denial brings with it emotional implications, causing people to have difficulty accepting moments in which uncertainty is present, not because it is bad or good in itself, but because our unawareness of it is such that we do not recognize the ups and downs that life brings and simply seek to protect ourselves from it by avoiding it.

Certainty and exclusivity are constantly represented in common sayings. A particular phrase is **"I like exclusivity. If what I can get from you, anyone can get, then I'm not interested."**, which not only reflects the clarity of the monogamous contract, the demand for fidelity and exclusivity, but also the rights given to the other over oneself, and at the same time, the renunciation to which each subject submits to comply with exclusivity. Likewise, one yields to this submission in order to acquire the certainty of reciprocal love—which, as we have already mentioned, will provide affective, social, and economic protection, and at the same time avoid going down unknown and probably uncontrollable paths.

Exclusivity is a way of experiencing our social, affective, and sexual relationships; this is learned and shared with other human beings. This is difficult to unlearn in couple relationships because it also implies removing a fundamental foundation for the maintenance of a romantic love bond. We are confronted with an issue that requires consideration from multiple perspectives, as well as questioning, because what is socially generalized or provides apparent certainty does not imply that it is the healthiest, provides greater welfare to humans, or is the only way to relate to one another lovingly.

Romantic Love and its Phrases

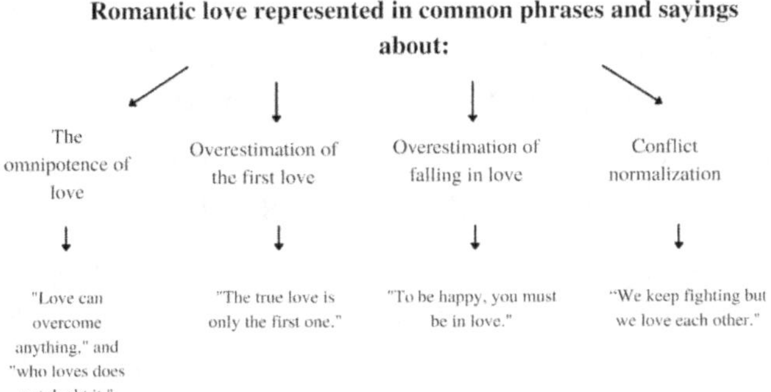

Omnipotence of Love

Romantic love is based on the need for total devotion to the other, the idealization of the couple, and the excessive romanticizing of feelings. The soul mate, the love of life, and the better half are symptoms (as if it were a social disease) of the transfiguration that the concept of love has undergone, which is shared and reproduced through the collective unconscious.

"Love can do anything", or a phrase more commonly adopted to describe romantic love, is: **"our love can do anything"**. It refers to the fact that we blindly believe in some supposed supernatural powers attributed to the feeling we experience as a couple, almost like a religion, since it is said that **"who loves does not doubt it".** This concept makes romantic love seem unquestionable, when in reality, it is valid and human to question what we live, experience, and feel, not only as a couple but in all aspects of life. In this sense, when one is under the influence of this perception and a part of the couple doubts about the relationship or their continuity in it, it is associated with the non-existence of "true love".

On the other hand, this type of belief also manifests itself as a kind of "faith" or confidence that the partner can modify certain behaviors or attitudes considered to be of little benefit to the members of the relationship and the relationship itself. "If he/she loves me, he/she will change" or " the love I feel for you will help me to change" are expressions that lead to perceiving love as a "remedy" or as the "antidote" for any evil that surrounds the couple under the justification of "it is possible, because we love each other." In other words, the fact of loving is enough to solve any problem.

These connotations of love and loving are adjusted to justify situations of violence, abuse, normalization of conflict, and also blackmail, since, when there is a transgression of the couple's agreements, the idea that "true love forgives/endures everything" and does not have the right to question itself may arise, leading to the resignation of being in an unbalanced relationship.

Overvaluation of First Love

In this section, we would like you to ask yourself the following question: Do you think that first love is as significant as they say it is?

It is easy to remember that first person with whom we discovered for the first time the bittersweet sensations of falling in love, the first passions, the encounters, the experiences, the discussions, and those unique details that we experienced in our first love life. In any case, this memory can be more or less unforgettable depending on the characteristics that were experienced in the course of the relationship and the way in which it ended.

However, we argue that there is an overvaluation of the first time in love when it is stated that **"true love is only the first one"** or **"like the first love, none"**. There are a few exceptions of people who met their partner in adolescence and were together their entire lives, but for the majority of us, the first love is just an idealization stored in the back of our minds.

The first love relationship is as important as the second, or third, or simply as the others that follow. We are likely to live them with great emotion and expectation because of our inexperience and the fact that they generally develop during our adolescence—a stage that is usually intense. In addition, it should be taken into account that there is no other relationship with which to compare it, and this probably makes it feel and be remembered as something more special.

Overvaluation of Falling in Love

We have already talked about love and infatuation, and about the positions that categorize them as different or equal. Likewise, the use of these words to describe feelings towards another person is frequent and normal in our society. Falling in love, punctually conceived as this chemical-hormonal process, is desired by most people because of the pleasant sensations and emotions it produces, as well as the prospect of well-being and the pleasure of living different experiences, especially with the person with whom one is in love.

This condition is usually extremely pleasurable and at the same time intense, which is the reason why we yearn so much to keep it. However, in this longing, we overvalue falling in love and associate it with positive meanings such as well-being, joy, and happiness. There are phrases used socially that reflect this: **"to be happy you have to be in love"** or **"to be in love is to find the right name for life"**. These phrases show how a higher value is given to the condition of being in love, since it is related to a life objective and, at the same time, the means to achieve it. In this sense, falling in love adopts an exaggerated expectation of what it can give us in life.

The aforementioned shows us that falling in love, in addition to producing chemical and hormonal sensations, implies the creation of meanings, associations, imaginaries, and longings about the affective human being's sphere. This becomes a term loaded with meaning not only neurological but also social, which constructs thoughts, feelings, and with them realities. The existence of an overvaluation of falling in love shows us how we have become attached to these meanings of falling in love itself and also how these meanings constitute who we are as social and sentient beings.

Conflict Normalization

Disagreements are common between people and in any type of relationship, including family, professional, friendship, and partnership, among others. We are constantly confronted with the otherness of an individual, animal, or thing that differs from our own characteristics and identity.

Human beings remain in a state of self-absorption since personal satisfaction and needs become the highest priority. This means that what is related to the other's priorities takes second place, since our own come first. By focusing on the personal—the self, the otherness and the complexities that also compose it are ignored. This ignorance leads to a lack of understanding of the life, social, and personal processes of others. At this point, it is easy not to seek to understand the other but to judge him/her from one's own perspective, and this is where the differences widen and extend into arguments and/or fights.

Couple relationships are the ones where arguments arise more frequently than any other kind of relationship since there is more regular sharing and disclosure of intimate aspects. From a psychological perspective, it is said that the other person is a mirror of oneself. Therefore, as the partner is one of the people with whom we spend the most time, this becomes a space for introspection, projection, and learning through that person we have in front of us.

The difficulty and the problem appear when the differences are reiterated and begin to become a frequent part of the relationship as if it were something normal. Regarding this, there are also common phrases like **"we keep arguing, but we love each other."** This phrase reflects how fights become part of the landscape of a love relationship because, by the fact that there exists love, the parties become abnegated, as it is a kind of renunciation of themselves to keep the love.

The types of phrases with this content are common in our daily lives, whether they come from familiar people or through media like radio or television. Knowing how to recognize them will help us to reflect on them and decide whether or not this is actually how we want to experience love as a couple.

Sexuality and its Phrases

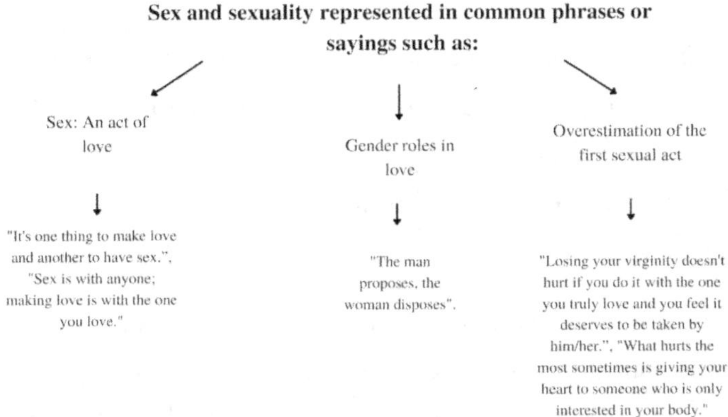

Sexuality does not escape the myths and idealizations that are held in regards to love, also because it is intermingled with some assumptions and/or taboos generated by this topic. For example, when it comes to sexual intercourse, a distinction is usually made as to whether it is carried out under the romantic model (romantic sexual intercourse) or if it is only for pleasure. In this situation, both positions usually have value judgments, but usually, people who enjoy sex aimed at the pursuit of pleasure are judged in greater proportion.

Although people who "make love" also intend to find pleasure in sex, the truth is that they tend to attribute to these sex-affective relationships characteristics such as better communication, greater stimulation, extension of time, emotional connection, and "magic," among others. While in sexual relationships for "simple pleasure", it is commonly stated that greater importance is given to the exploration of the other body, its excitability, and as the main objective to achieve orgasm. For these reasons, it is common to hear phrases such as **"It's one thing to make love and another to have sex." and "Sex is with anyone; making love is with the one you love."**

Following this same line, we find the **overvaluation of the first sexual act** closely related to the idea/idealization of **first love**. In this overvaluation, "virginity" is attributed to the characteristic of an offering or gift of the highest value, especially from a **woman** to a man.

What is not explored is that behind this "gift", which is usually related to the pain and sacrifice of women and which is associated with the alleged "rupture of the hymen", is a belief strongly rooted in religion and patriarchy. For centuries, with the reproduction of the concept of "virginity", women have been strongly judged for losing this "social value" when they have decided to have their first sexual act before marriage, or in other cases, for doing it without loving the person.

To better illustrate what is meant, we use the following phrase as an example: **"Losing your virginity does not hurt if you do it with someone you really love and you feel it deserves to be taken by him/her".** Despite the great achievements of the feminist movement and the famous sexual revolution in vogue of maximum enjoyment of sex and equal access to it, other kinds of phrases or statements that persist in romanticizing the sexual act, but also in making sexual differentiations that grant predetermined standards and roles according to gender, continue to be reproduced.

Regarding the previous point, we find phrases such as **"the man proposes, the woman disposes"** that evidence the establishment of specific roles within courtship. Despite the fact that this has been deconstructed and more and more we find sex-affective relationships in which men and women depart from behaviors determined by their gender, even today the repetition of these sayings continues, which limits the behavior of each subject in front of the person he/she likes. In this way, sexist and chauvinist judgments are repeated, in which women are expected to depend on a man's initiative in order to be able to engage in the practice of their sensuality and sexuality.

In our society, there are judgments and discriminations against women that change the imaginary that covers the aforementioned phrase, because she is labeled as "easy" or "slutty" in her act of proposal and initiative. The same thing happens to men who break with the paradigm that they are the ones who should be the proposers and initiate the approach to a woman, since they are often subjected to comments that question their sexual orientation or are criticized as passive or "timorous." As can be observed, the phrase "the man proposes and the woman disposes" contains violent and discriminatory elements towards heterosexual men and women, and also towards people who identify themselves as homosexuals, since it excludes the possibility of this type of sexual-affective relationship. By only mentioning man-woman, it is taken for granted that this is the only form of courtship and of being in a couple, since it does not contemplate the other possibilities of relating in love.

Reflections on the Phrases

Which of these phrases do you remember having used or having heard from someone close or unknown to you? Regardless of the phrase you have encountered in your life and how it occurred, we recommend that before using any of these or other phrases that circulate in social spaces, you pause to consider what you are going to say and what you truly want to say, what message you are sending to that person, and what you are offering to society with your specific act or saying. Many times, we believe that what we speak and say is not so significant, but this is a big mistake, because the words themselves build realities not only for you or the people around you, but also in the social world you cohabit.

Everything you see around you is part of a social creation that was made possible by its dissemination through language. Therefore, to enable a less biased and less coercive society, every human being can start with him/herself, reviewing what he/she thinks and says through his/her speech. Since this becomes part of the beliefs and ways of assuming and living life.

For this reason, the exposure of these phrases is not done without intentionality. On the contrary, it is done with a clear purpose, and that is to deconstruct what we believe to be unquestionable or normal. For this purpose, in this chapter we "drill" ideas anchored in our minds that do little to help us in public social relationships or more intimate ones such as those of a couple. But how can we think and live outside of the social and cultural norms surrounding love, the couple, and sexuality? We will seek to answer this complex question in the following chapter, of course, in a purposeful way, which can provide us with alternative elements to experience our sexual-affective relationships in a different way.

REBUILDING OTHER WAYS
OF LOVING

CHAPTER IV: PRACTICES FOR A DISRUPTIVE LOVE OF THE NORM

We have seen love as a couple as a social construction in which standardizations, ideals, and expectations that have been collectively built around the notion of romantic love are easily seen, and how this, far from being a source of personal and sexual wellbeing, has become a root of conflicts and anxiety for people. Likewise, social forms characterized by family and monogamy have been created, which have made love part of the gear of the economic system in which we are immersed.

In spite of what was mentioned above, as emotional beings, we recognize that it is difficult to get out of these social dynamics and we understand love as something fundamental for human beings, perhaps since the dawn of their existence. For thousands of years, we have developed this form of close and intimate connection with each other, and it has constituted and configured us as human beings.

However, this section is designed to ensure that these love experiences as a couple are not traumatic for any member of the relationship; with this, we hope to make practical suggestions for how to relate to each other as a couple in ways other than the hegemonic one in order to love more consciously.

Before starting with our proposals, we believe that it is important that, at the moment of starting a relationship, each party should expose in a transparent way the characteristics and elements that they are looking for in a partner and explicitly state the conditions under which the agreement between the parties will be made, that is, to make clear under what concepts they are going to relate to each other. Some elements to consider would be: the level of commitment they intend to establish, the limits of fidelity, if they are looking for a monogamous or open relationship, etc.

It is essential that before entering into a relationship, each subject reflects on whether he/she is really able and willing to comply with what is being agreed upon, so that based on this decision, he/she can decide whether to commit to the relationship or not, since, once the agreement has been made, the expectation is that it will be respected. Many of the problems in relationships are associated with non-compliance with agreements, although most of these are not made explicit at the beginning of the relationship and are usually taken for granted.

Spaces of Encounter

Up to this point, an approach has been made to the elements that constitute and conceal what we socially name as a couple. From this, we allow ourselves in the following points to develop some proposals aimed at exercising a different form of relationship in the couple, which can disrupt certain aspects that we have integrated from romantic love, monogamy, and sexuality. As we have seen, some of the elements that we have been taught about relationships and love as a couple are harmful to our personal and social world.

It should be emphasized that the following proposals acknowledge and recognize the importance of a partner for modern human beings, which is why they do not aim to eliminate or totally detonate this form of relationship, but rather to provide people who decide to relate in this way with other forms of bonding that allow them to let go of the dynamics of possessiveness, standardization, and symbolic violence, and at the same time, make possible a less harmful form of bonding for the parties.

We are aware that the idea of living "love as a couple" will not cease to exist since it is a quite normalized way of assuming this human experience. For this reason, we consider it important to provide other tools that allow us to free ourselves from social ties and demands that hurt us and sometimes make us sick by assuming this symbolization of the couple and many other ways of relating to each other in society.

Spending a lot of time with a person is usually associated with sharing, although this does not necessarily mean real sharing. Since you can be with someone in many spaces, but you may not be present and not generate a bond with them. As an example, that parent who thinks he or she spends time with a child because they are together at home, but each one is watching a different TV program or is entertained on social networks. In these cases, there is no integration and bonding with each other, nor a consensus of shared activities or tastes. For this reason, we have focused this section on generating spaces for encounters because we understand the word "encounter" as a space for people to get together, in which they interact and build relationships.

Under this conception, in an encounter, human beings engage in dialogue, approach each other and get closer. To encourage this type of dynamic in a couple relationship, we consider some actions that allow the encounter with the other. Those are:

Actions of " Negativity"

For the author, Byung-Chul Han, the actions of negativity are those in which the human being detaches himself from productive activities, allowing himself to rest in body and mind, reconnecting with other fundamental aspects of the subject. Among these activities, we can suggest the following to be done as a couple:

- Meditation, both together and individually
- Kundalini Yoga practiced both together and separately
- Activities in natural environments
- Relaxation, activities such as massages and aromatherapy

Actions of Movement

Movement actions refer to those that involve the bodies. These are useful because they allow that physical part that enables us to participate in this particular materiality to feel active for the benefit of itself and not only for economic productivity.

- Activities that involve the body, such as sports, art, and games.
- Leisure and entertainment activities depend on the preferences of the people in the relationship. They can be analyzed and allowed to explore activities that are pleasant and fun to share. There are those who prefer to go to the theater, as well as others who choose to go out to eat, have cocktails or go to a café.

Both negative and movement actions make it possible to connect with our own bodies and minds, but also with those of the people we share these activities with, since they allow us to be more present and connect us with the experience we are having. In addition, it facilitates the development of feelings of peace and tranquility, which are beneficial not only for each human being but also so that the emotional bonds and relationships that we establish are more comprehensive. In this way, we seek that otherness matters, it means equality and the undervaluation of the other is less recurrent.

This also makes it possible to teach and learn about the other and about oneself, from preferences to capacities, difficulties and other aspects; this possibility of learning can be enhanced by means of dialogue. The latter is another practice that we consider, from our perspective, useful for the reelaboration of a couple with more reflective and understanding elements regarding otherness and the self. As a result, the following section focuses on the development of this as a practice for a more unconventional couple relationship.

Connect and Understand Each Other

Dialogue practice is usually one of the first tools recommended to maintain any kind of stable, "healthy" and balanced relationship, in such a way that sometimes it loses its value by seeming like a cliché. Much is said and written on the subject, both in books and on the web. However, we find that there is no further study beyond highlighting its importance and offering some abstract exercises in which the couple can practice this increasingly scarce communicative skill.

From our perspective, we want to encourage you to review the following ideas that can strengthen your current or future relationship with simple exercises that can help you and your partner bond as a team with a shared language and symbology, and in this way, create trust, connection, and empathy.

From Monologue to Dialogue, Dialogue to Silence

How many of the people with whom you think you are having a dialogue or a conversation, talk incessantly and also seem to pay little or no attention to the details of the interventions you make? And has it ever happened to you that when you are arguing with someone, you don't listen to what the person is saying because you are thinking ahead about what you are going to say?

Dialogue is based on feedback between the people who are interacting with each other. This implies fully listening to the other person, with genuine interest, overcoming the temptation of anchoring oneself in a monologue where only one of the parties expresses himself/herself. In the case of romantic relationships, dialogue is the appropriate practice to get to know the partner a little better, to identify and understand his/her way of thinking, and to express emotions that are kept bottled up for lack of active listening.

Ideas for Strengthening Dialogue With your Partner

- Try to create moments to talk about the relationship: Do you remember how you met? What did each of you think and feel about the other? Do you remember how you dressed on your first date? What other things caught your attention during your first encounters? Tell each other in detail the other side of the story and how each of you experienced it. This will generate more sympathy and complicity in the relationship.
- Other questions to ask about the relationship can be aimed at knowing how they feel now inside it, how they have felt, what they expect from it, what they like and what they don't like that much.
- Acknowledge each other's emotions. If your partner confesses to you that something X or Y makes him/her feel a certain way, acknowledge it as a valid emotion because undervaluing feelings or emotions undoes our empathy as well as trust in our relationships. Just as it is essential to listen to your partner's feelings and fears, it is essential that you also recognize yours without minimizing them and express them assertively.
- Talking about each other as individuals, about personal concerns and one's own experiences in the different spheres that we socially occupy, allows us to understand the other person's humanity and also reveals points that we have in common, such as fears, experiences, expectations, and emotions.

- Giving each other moments of silence is also part of the dialogue, allowing reflection and taking a break from verbalization and compulsive thinking.

Discussing is Different from Fighting

We agree with many relationship experts when they say that arguing is not the same as fighting. To put it in a nutshell, arguing means the peaceful, although perhaps a little passionate, exchange of opposing opinions that, at some point, may or may not coincide, depending on the arguments used. However, some couple discussions end in fights, with the couple losing respect and control. Shouting, slaps, and hurtful phrases, among others, can be used in an attempt to be right, superimposing one's own opinion over that of the other person.

Wounds resulting from fights often create resentment and a desire for revenge, deteriorating the strength of the couple and breaking the connection you have with that person. For this reason, we propose some insights on how to discuss this in a more constructive way.

- To learn how to discuss, create, or generate spaces for debate. Question current or past topics of interest in a critical way, giving your opinion about them and counter-arguing what the other person says, all in a serene and calm manner. This is an exercise in argumentation and building discussion skills.
- Abandon the idea of being right. "Being right" is a trick of the ego, which does not bring any benefit and places us in competition with the person we claim to love.

- Establish and maintain balance in the responsibilities of the relationship at the economic, emotional, domestic (distribution of tasks), parenting, etc. level.
- Never use elements of personal and intimate aspects that the partner has confided in to win an argument.
- It is important to keep in balance other components of non-verbal communication: postures, gestures, tone of voice, etc.
- Beware of interpretations. As human beings absorbed in culture and possessing social and individual subjectivity, we produce symbols and emotions according to our lived experiences. It is relevant that, when in doubt about the partner's thoughts and feelings, we ask adequate and concrete questions to really know what is going on, thus omitting our value judgments and false interpretations of reality.
- Reinforce the intention to want to be well as a couple with simple words that at the same time recharge the relationship: I'm sorry, excuse me, I was wrong, thank you, I love you, among others.

As we have seen, there are different resources that can be adopted and combined to build more solid communication and dialogue. Using creativity is essential to find and create other elements in order to strengthen the bond and the connection that the couple is looking for.

Less Stereotyped Sexual Experiences

We may or may not agree that sexuality itself is each person's responsibility, because on one hand, we are socially and culturally molded, and on the other hand, we are the ones who have the opportunity to make of our sexuality a space of resistance and creativity.

As we have emphasized during the development of this book, behind those places that we believe to be intimate and personal, there is a type of structure or social control. Although perhaps no one has designed it in detail, the truth is that structure has been implanted in our contexts and fulfills some functions, such as maintaining certain orders and delegating duties, that give meaning to our social and economic organization. This happens with romantic love, monogamy, and sexuality. Regarding the last one, culturally we have the idea that it is lived in a specific way. Thus, sexuality is associated with concepts of genitality, heteronormativity, sexual roles, and myths learned from the pornography industry.

How long should a sexual encounter last and in this, how many orgasms should a person have? How big should a man's penis be to satisfy his partner? How often should they have sexual encounters? If they don't have enough sex, then there is no love?

All these questions evoke a "normality" learned precisely from these social and cultural structures that encourage the standardization of sexual acts, making the concept of sexuality a mathematical formula that must have constant "parts" and symbols in order to ensure the same type of result.

Cecilia Ce, psychologist and sexology specialist, shares with us an outline of what she considers to be the prevailing "equation" or "formula" of sexuality, stereotyped and implanted in our collective unconscious:

$$\left[20' \bullet P \left(\frac{Pe}{V} \right) = OH! \right]$$

Where:

$'$ = time (minutes)

P = Penetration

Pe = Penis

V = Vagina

OH! = Orgasm

As can be seen, in this mathematical function, everything is standardized. In sexual intercourse, there is an excess of measurement, both of the time spent on this activity as well as the counting of orgasms; this is something frequently exhibited by men to demonstrate their ability to satisfy women. Also, it is possible to read between the lines what is understood as "normal" when taking for granted that sexual relationships have to be between a man and a woman, or better, between a vagina and a penis. On the other hand, overvalued penetration is observed as the only means of achieving the ultimate goal: orgasm. This has become the obsession of many, who see it as the only destination and meaning of sexual intercourse.

From this perspective, we could ask ourselves: To what extent are we the owners and creators of our erotic desires? Where is the limit within the prevailing conditions?

On the other hand, there is a small gap in our resistance to the stereotypes and standardizations that have somehow conditioned us. That is where we can embrace the responsibility of our own sexuality, understanding that in this context, "normality" is relative and that there may be as many normalities as there are people and couples, thanks to the codes and symbols that are established.

Because we find a little more freedom when we leave the sexuality norm, this resistance implies a loss of the desire to maintain control. This is an invitation to understand our erogenous zones beyond genitality and orgasm as something more than an end. In the same way, we emphasize that it is fundamental to create spaces for the self-recognition of one's own sexuality and the recognition of what the other person likes and what he/she does not like, through the exploration of body and desire, either together or separately. This is possible to try through masturbation.

Finally, and most importantly of all, sexual relationships must always be consensual, or they must not be.

Appropriating the Personal Process

Social interaction is a fundamental element for human beings since it allows them to construct their own subjectivity, integrate mental structures, and adapt to the social structures that affect them. In this sense, social interaction participates not only in the construction of identities but also in the preservation of certain forms of social organization, since it enables the creation, participation, and reproduction of the symbolic world in which we human beings move and develop. In other words, social relationships are an essential part of humanity since, besides allowing us to establish contact with others, they also contribute to our constitution as particular subjects.

Couple relationships are built on constant interaction with an "exclusive" other. Therefore, it is common and fundamental to carry out an approach to solve problems in couples, including both parties involved. However, from our position, we consider that this is not the only way to practice a disruptive relationship to the hegemonic learned one, since other practices can be articulated focused on the individual reflection of each of the parts of the couple. This is important to create an appropriation of the personal process and allow them to be less dependent on the partner.

Among these practices we propose the following:

Spaces for Being Alone

Being alone or in solitude generally has a negative connotation since it is usually associated with failure and other aspects categorized as negative, such as boredom and sadness. However, in these states, there are unknown elements that can provide several lessons, especially about ourselves. For this, we propose that we allow ourselves to create spaces where we can be alone and do activities that we enjoy and connect with. To discover what these are, it is necessary to provide us with a space to recognize our personal interests, then make room for them and allow us to materialize these preferences. Try in these spaces to let go of thoughts about "what people will say when they see you alone". Focus on you and what you have decided to do for yourself. In this way, you may discover or develop new skills or explore other social contexts.

We also consider it fundamental within these spaces to create moments not only of interest but also of reflection that allow us to deeply think and feel ourselves. This is in order to connect with our desires but also with disturbances that are important to transcend or transform in order to be different individuals with less suffering and limitations. This type of space is proposed to be channeled by recognition and understanding and not by judgment. Because we will not seek self-criticism or create feelings of guilt or frustration in this manner, but rather seek to understand the reason for our ways of being, feeling, and acting. This practice is useful so that in this encounter with the other, we become more understanding subjects of our own humanity and that of the one we have in front of us.

- Considerations for these personal spaces, to work on ourselves as subjects and as subjects in a couple:

Recommendations in Case of Recurrent Jealousy

Try to understand that the other person does not belong to you, nor do you belong to him/her (even if you call each other "my boyfriend/girlfriend" or "my spouse"). Before they met, they were subjects that did not belong to anyone, and neither do they belong to anyone now that they are a couple. The difference is that now they decide to share affective and sexual spaces. Although this or any other situation does not give you the right to believe you are a person's owner, because people are not objects, we are complex beings that are neither owned nor lost.

Also, try to remember in these spaces of solitude, to keep in mind how you feel when you allow yourself to be dominated by jealousy. The evocation of these sensations can allow you to recognize the pain, damage, and affectation that you get when jealousy dominates you. Reflect on it. If you consider it relevant to talk about it, look for the most appropriate words to express the insecurity you experience to your partner.

In these spaces of sharing with yourself, you will begin to work on these fixed ideas about the possession of that other person who is your partner. We suggest that, if you have difficulties with jealousy, avoid exerting control over your partner. For example, do not check his/her cell phone, do not ask him/her to share the location of the place where he/she is, do not forbid meetings with friends, or wear a certain clothing style, among others.

It is essential to provide spaces for reflection on the behaviors of insecurity and jealousy that we sometimes experience, in order to offer other possibilities that bring us closer to creating feelings of security based on ourselves and not on what our partner does or does not do.

- Recommendations in Cases of Experiencing Expectations About Received Love

As we explain throughout the book, we have learned through society some specific ways of relating affectively, which leads us to expect one or some specific ways of acting from the person with whom we share the monogamous "contract". In the face of this, it is expected to show affection in X or Y way, leaving out of sight other expressions that were not learned but that for a particular subject can mean giving something important of himself/herself. Reflection on this allows us to express our feelings in the way we feel but also understand the other's way of giving love.

At this point, it is important to know how to discern between those "signs of affection" that camouflage harmful situations and actions for the parties, since different acts of violence are allowed in the name of love. It is essential to know how to differentiate, since actions that restrict, hurt, or violate the body or psyche of people, beyond showing affection, show us possible justifications in the name of love.

- Recommendations in Cases of Experiencing Frustration for not Having a Partner

It is complex not to experience the desire to have a partner when we have seen that society tells us through various means that it is normal and essential to have one. However, going deeper into the fact that these are precisely the issues that society itself invented to mold us into specific ways of relating can allow you to pause and ask yourself if you really want to be in a relationship or if it is something that has been imposed on you by your family or your social environment. Around the answer you find, you will begin to understand why this aspect is essential for you, and thus avoid looking for a partner in "automatic mode". It would be more beneficial to pause when deciding whether or not to be in a relationship based on your reflection, so that you do not make decisions without knowing what drives you to choose them or what is behind them.

- Recommendations in Cases of Judgment and Victimization

Do not put yourself in the position of believing you are superior or inferior. This is fundamental in order not to distort the facts that may happen in a couple. Therefore, do not try to place yourself with the "gift" of reason or be the victim who has no responsibility for the events that happen. Assuming responsibility entails refraining from any identification (judgment or victimization), which may enable you to position yourself in a less dramatic and punishing manner, for a more committed, responsible, and understanding relationship with yourself and the other person.

- Build Social Spaces With Other People

The spheres in which the human being develops are diverse; therefore, to consider that the partner covers everything is a mistake. It is important that both parties can create spaces to share with other subjects for personal fulfillment, because, as mentioned at the beginning of this section, social interaction is fundamental for the construction of each human being.

Other social relationships such as professional, friendship, or family relationships offer different spaces to the individual, which serve as support in the case of a breakup or in situations of personal or couple difficulties. Spaces with other people provide growth because they allow getting to know other realities, interests, and perspectives from which the relationship can also benefit.

- Recommendations that Can Enhance Solo Spaces

- Attend psychotherapy
- Read the guide 4 Formas de Conocerte en tu Proceso Humano

www.GuiaParaSerHumanos.com/descargar-gratis/

Conclusion of this point: take possession of your own "freedom" and not that of the other.

Conclusions

Couple relationships are much more than what is superficially perceived. As can be seen, there are deep and hidden elements that influence and integrate them, which makes them function under the articulated dynamics of exclusivity, romanticism, and heteronormativity. These aspects not only condition our sex-affective relationships but also shape our desires, beliefs, and feelings as individual and social subjects.

The understanding of monogamy, romantic love, and sexuality as fundamental pillars of couple relationships from a reflective-critical perspective makes it possible to begin more conscious paths and processes of change not only for current couples, but also for those who will be established in the future or for people who decide to be alone.

Changing the way we relate to each other as a couple implies will, patience, and understanding from and for both parties. Since these are aspects that have crossed us for almost all our lives, they have a high degree of complexity to transform them. However, with a willing and conscious practice of the actions proposed in the last chapter, it is possible to rebuild our love relationships in different and alternative ways, allowing us to bond in healthier, less possessive, and coercive ways, as well as to accept ourselves and otherness in all its diversity and all its nuances.

Glossary

Commoditization: Refers to how, under the economic model of capitalism, human feelings, emotions, relationships, behaviors, culture, and knowledge take the form of merchandise and/or products available for sale or to be marketed for consumption.

Deconstruct: A process through which an individual, couple, or group of people recognize, question, and risk breaking down the imaginaries, judgments, stereotypes, beliefs, and meanings learned and assumed as "truth" and "normal".

Ego: It is the non-conscious belief that the true self is the physical, mental, or emotional "I". This posture generates an identification with one's own mind and thoughts about oneself, creating a false sense of being, separated from other living and non-living beings that are part of a whole.

Heteronormativity: Is a generalized social concept and practice that accepts the feminine role for bodies born with vagina and the masculine role for bodies born with penis as natural and normal, and with it, attraction between people is given in a heterosexual way, without acknowledging other diverse sexual ways of being.

Idealize: To exaggerate and extol the virtues of a situation, person, or thing while downplaying or ignoring its flaws.

Ideology: The ideas and beliefs of a group of people or a social, political, religious, or other movement that seeks to superimpose and legitimize the ideas in which it believes and the power of the group or movement that defends them.

Imperative: Hidden social mandates and orders that impose the actions and attitudes expected of people.

Introspection: It is a process in which a person reviews his or her emotional and mental states, as well as his or her history and present while being honest, in order to know and question himself or herself.

Moralizing: It is the action of judging as good or bad acts, decisions, opinions, among others. It is common for religious discourses and ideologies to frequently make this type of judgment.

Normalize: A way in which, through social pressure, repetition, and ideology, certain ideas, behaviors, and procedures are taken for granted and accepted as "natural" and unquestionable.

Otherness: A term used mainly in the social and human sciences to refer to the phenomenon of the "other": Through the recognition of the other's existence, we reaffirm our own identity. To understand the other is to know ourselves and who we are.

Re-elaborate: To give deeper meaning to concepts and ideas about which a norm or imaginary has been established about oneself or the world around one.

Rebuild: A process articulated to deconstruction, in which after questioning preconceptions, a path is undertaken to create new meanings, taking into account what has been learned and acknowledging the limitations generated by what was believed to be normal and true.

Romantic love: It is a cultural, social, and economic construction that has created homogeneous ways of behaving, feeling, and living love as a couple.

Sexist: It is the discrimination and division between genders (feminine and masculine) that leads to unequal relations between men and women. This discrimination affects both genders, but historically, it has primarily affected women and issues concerning women.

Social Construction: A shared perspective about the world that is created and constructed through the interaction and interrelation of a group of people about external events and the ways in which human beings should act, feel, and think.

Social Reproduction: It is a social process through which historically dominant power, economic, political, and cultural structures are transmitted.

Stereotypes: Are socioculturally constructed and learned beliefs that seek to classify the external and internal human worlds. This classification generates arbitrary divisions and limitations of superiority and inferiority according to what it is classified as (gender, race, physique, etc.).

Symbolic Violence: This is a type of violence hidden and invisible in human actions, discourse, and norms that produces social relations of power and leads to situations of inequality and discrimination. This is accepted as "normal", without being questioned or refuted.

To make visible: Making historical, social, and cultural dynamics visible in people or groups of people who are disadvantaged and/or vulnerable.

Bibliography

Ce, C. (2019). La ecuación del Sexo. https://www.ted.com/talks/ cecilia_ce_la_ecuacion_del_sexo?language=es, Rosario, Argentina.

Chul Han, B. (2010). La sociedad del cansancio.

Chul Han, B. (2012). *La agonia del Eros*.

Correa Román, J. (2018). La deconstrucción del amor como imperativo ético. *Ensayos de filosofía*.

Engels, F. (1980). *El Origen de la familia, la propiedad privada y el estado*.

Foucault, M. (1991). *Historia de la Sexualidad I La Voluntad del Saber*.

Platón. (1871). El Banquete. Edición de Patricia de Azcarate. Tomo 5.

Plutchik, R. (1987). Las emociones.

Reidl Martinez, L. (2005). Celos y envidia: emociones humanas.

Rosillo, E. (2017). El amor que nos venden las canciones. *La Marea*.

Sztajnszrajber, D. (s.f.). ¿Se puede salir de la monogamia? https:// www.youtube.com/watch?v=uCmOd2fncGY, Argentina.

Author's Recommendations

Dear Reader,

We appreciate the time dedicated to reading this work, and we hope that it will be useful in your life as a couple. Preferably, if you are in a relationship, it is recommended that it be read by both of you, since in this way you will be able to discuss the contents and learn about how social phenomena cohabit within the relationship.

In addition, we recommend psychological accompaniment with a critical-social approach that helps the couple to understand their own realities and collaborate in the creation of tools that allow them to find greater satisfaction within the relationship without losing sight of the subjects as social beings.

You can complement the present book with the free guide "**4 formas de conocerte en tu proceso humano**" that you will find on our website, through the following link: www.guia-paraserhumanos.com/descargar-gratis/.

On our website, www.guiaparaserhumanos.com, you will also find various instruments for a comprehensive understanding of the human process, such as a blog, guides, books, courses, and individual and couple psychological therapy.

If you liked this book, we encourage you to support us with a review on Amazon. It would help us more than you think.

Thanks again for your support;

The authors

About the Authors

From the social categories, I am Jenny Paola Osorio Echeverri, a Psychologist with a critical approach, a specialist and a candidate for a Master's degree in Educational Innovation.

I feel a strong social commitment. I believe that situations have backgrounds that need to be recognized in the personal and spiritual spheres in order to transform societies into more reflective and conscious ones.

From social labels: I am Carolina Cardona, International Business Administrator and candidate for a Master's degree in Latin American Studies.

I am intrigued by the relationships we have with other living beings, as well as the origins and anthropological evolution of human beings. I have 6 years of experience supporting people with the work burdens generated by our society.

www.GuiaParaSerHumanos.com

 facebook.com/GuiaparaSerHumanos2021

 twitter.com/HumanosGuia

 instagram.com/guiaparaserhumanos

9 789584 969071